THE BADGICORN

Sam Haynes

Illustrated by Sam Dunn

For Darcey & Avery

"Everybody is a genius. But if you judge a fish by its ability to climb a tree, it will live its whole life believing that it is stupid."

- Anonymous

In a deep, dark hole, beneath bracken and thorns,
you might find the burrow of the Badgicorn.
Not unicorn or badger, but in-between.
A little bit weird, but much more than he seems.

He has a black and white body, plump and squat,
with a unicorn's head plonked crudely on top.
Though he looks a bit silly, you'll often find
that creatures half as pretty are twice as kind.

The unicorns filled him with terrible dread.
All the myths and legends had gone to their heads!
So when he saw them gathered in a clearing,
he silently tiptoed beyond their hearing.

He was almost away, he was almost free,
but a branch had fallen from an old oak tree.
He trod on the branch and it broke with a crunch...
and a unicorn looked up from her packed lunch.

'Badgicorn, Badgicorn, now what's the hurry?
There's really no need to scrabble and scurry.'
The Badgicorn groaned, feeling very awkward,
as the unicorn grinned and sauntered forward.

'From your neck to your horn, we're almost the same,
so we hoped you might join in our simple game.
Go on, little one, don't hide under your paw.
Watch me summon the spring to the forest floor.'

The unicorn whinnied, then bent her head low
and she blew on the ground and asked it to grow.
The empty earth trembled, and before their eyes
rose a carpet of bluebells and butterflies.

The fairy folk gathered on their fairy hill.
'Come on,' they said, *'let's see the Badgicorn's skill.'*
The Badgicorn gasped, he was very impressed.
'I've not done it before, but I'll do my best.'

He blew on the grass till it tickled his nose,
and begged it for tulips or a single rose.
But as he struggled and strained to prove his worth,
black, razor-sharp thorns twisted out of the earth.

The unicorn laughed as she took in the scene,
'Well, that's the foulest bouquet I've ever seen!'
As the Badgicorn frowned and tried to sneak by,
another approached with a glint in his eye.

'I'm a blue belt in Rainbows,' he said with glee.
'Can you light up the sky with such artistry?'
A flick of his horn and a flick of his hair
sent a river of colour into the air.

The pixies went *'AWWW!'* and the yetis went *'OOOO!'*
'Come on,' they said, *'what can a Badgicorn do?'*
The Badgicorn paled, and he said with a sigh,
'I really don't know, but I'll give it a try.'

But the Badgicorn didn't know where to start.
He knew more about slugs than great works of art.
He started to sweat and he started to shake,
with no idea what kind of rainbow he'd make.

Then out of his horn, with a terrible crash,
came rumbles of thunder and a blinding flash.
Then dark storm clouds gathered and billowed around,
as a shower of raindrops splashed on the ground.

The unicorns jeered, *'Oh no, what a muddle!'*
and fell about laughing in muddy puddles.
The Badgicorn sniffed, his eyes starting to well,
'I can't even manage the easiest spell...'

But a unicorn pleaded, *'Don't say goodbye.*
I have one for you that's as easy as pie.'
She spotted a lizard and ushered it near,
then put her head next to its tiny green ear.

'I'll grant you a wish. What's your deepest desire?'
'Oooh!' said the lizard, *'I would like to breathe fire!'*
As the unicorn nodded, her eyes shone bright,
and her great horn shimmered like pearls in the light.

Then the lizard grew vast, and great wings spread out,
and flames flickered out of the end of its snout.
A coven of witches applauded in awe,
and cackled, *'Dear Badgicorn, give us one more!*

'I wish for magical shoes of ruby red.
Please fashion me some with that horn on your head.'
So he pictured sparkles, like dew in the dawn,
and tried to shape it into a foot-like form.

But instead of crafting some ruby slippers,
he covered her toes in flopping wet kippers.
The whole forest laughed, and they rolled on the floor,
until the former-lizard opened his jaw.

He devoured the kippers with a fearsome growl,
as the wicked witch cowered under her cowl.
Then he took to the air with a dreadful roar,
and a column of fire burst out of its maw.

And the unicorns knew the mistake they'd made,
as dragon-fire raged through the Enchanted Glade.
The forest was screaming: *'He has to be stopped!'*
as the unicorns fainted and promptly dropped.

The Badgicorn suddenly had an idea.
'There is a magical cave not far from here!'
He ran to the cave and focussed his power,
and kippers rose up in a giant tower.

The smell was so great it rose up to the clouds,
and a great belly rumbled terribly loud.
The dragon flew down for his favourite dish.
How could he resist such a mountain of fish?

As he roared through the cave to begin his feast,
the Badgicorn thought: *I can do this, at least...*
He spoke to the earth and he brandished his horn,
and covered the entrance with thickets and thorns.

The dragon was trapped, but the forest still burned,
and so back to the blazing woods he returned.
The Badgicorn reared up, confronting the flames,
then uttered a spell, and with his horn, took aim.

He'd done it before and could do so again,
with all of his magic he'd summon the rain.
The wildfire drew closer, it flared and it spread
as the storm clouds billowed and swirled overhead.

Thick and fast the rain fell, coming to their aid.
Thick and fast it poured upon the burning glade.
When the last ember died and the black smoke cleared,
the Badgicorn emerged and the forest cheered.

They rushed out to greet him, the dryads and fauns,
and the unicorns humbly lowered their horns.
'I'm sorry we teased you, we've all been so blind.
We're honoured to count you as one of our kind!'

He realised then, and he never forgot,
you shouldn't pretend to be something you're not.
He said with a smile, as he raised up his horn,
'I'm not a unicorn. I'm the Badgicorn!'

Printed in Great Britain
by Amazon